Book Design: Aaron & Michelle Grayum - The Gray Umbrella, LLC
Front & Back Cover Design and Nerve / Heart Artwork: Tracy Baskette Fleaner
Photography: Becky Fluke / Blu Sanders / Miranda Lambert
Logos and additional art: Loni Carr - The Whiskey Ginger

NOTICE
Mention of specific companies, organizations, or authorities in this book
does not imply endorsement by the author or publisher, nor does mention of specific companies,
organizations, or authorities imply that they endorse this book, its author, or the publisher.

www.Mirandalambert.com
Printed in the U.S.A.

$ US 30.00
MUSIC

NAME: Miranda

The weight of
these wings

- a wish to fly
- a wish to feel your
  feet on the ground

a six foot span
with a gust of
wind

a six foot span
in a hard rain

when the clouds let go
and the water covers
the feathers

when the clouds part
and the sun dries
the tears

a dream to move
people with words
a dream to be
heard

a megaphone, a micr~~

from megaphone to
muchrophone

from a scream to
a whisper.

THE NERVE:

one of the many thin parts that control
movement and feeling by carrying
messages between the brain and other
parts of the body
  : the rude attitude of someone who says
or does things that make other people
angry or upset
  : courage that allows you to do
something that is dangerous, difficult,
or frightening:
   Source: Merriam-Webster's

... The nerve that transmits pain
The nerve to say Goodbye
The nerve to follow your heart
The nerve to be alone ... with you
The nerve to be happy

light.

The Nerve

- the hands shake while lighting a cigarette
- The sigh, but not of relief

- The eyes twitch not knowing if they are open or closed, they wander

- The mind races through the night stopping only to count the times the chain hits the globe on the ceiling fan. Clink clink clink in almost perfect time.

- The drive... how much longer... are we there yet... will we ever really get there

Runnin' Just In Case

Miranda Lambert/Gwen Sebastian (BMI/ASCAP)

There's trouble where I'm going but I'm gonna go there anyway
I hate Sunday mornings 'cause they always seem to start this way
I'm lookin' for a lighter, I already bought the cigarettes
Guess I picked me up a habit on my way out of Lafayette

East bound and down, I turn it up 'cause that's sure how I feel
My mind is racing through the pines, my hands are shaky on this steering wheel
I'm goin' north on 59 but I know good and well I'm headed south
'Cause me and Birmingham don't have a history of working out

What I lost in Louisiana
I found back in Alabama
But nobody ever taught me how to stay
It ain't love that I'm chasin'
But I'm runnin' just in case

I ain't unpacked my suitcase since the day that I turned 21
It's been a long 10 years since then, it's gettin' kinda cumbersome
The first one, and the last one, and the one that's got my name in ink
The smoker, and the fighter, and the one in every song I sing

What I lost in Lubbock, Texas
I looked for in all the rest
But I guess no one ever taught me how to stay
It ain't love that I'm chasin'
But I'm runnin' just in case

I carry them around with me, I don't mind havin' scars
Happiness ain't prison but there's freedom in a broken heart

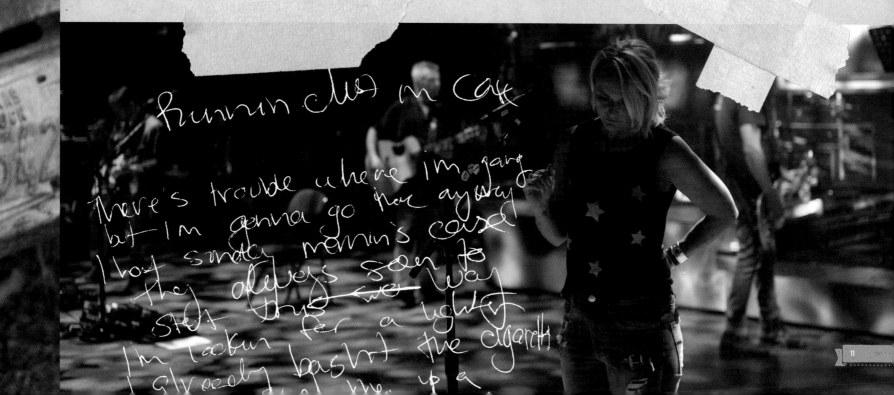

Highway Vagabond

Luke Dick/Natalie Hemby/Shane McAnally (BMI/GMR)

I wanna go somewhere where nobody knows
I wanna know somewhere where nobody goes
Following gold lines on the ground, northbound, southbound
There's something about the way I feel when the wheels go 'round and around and around

Chorus 1:
Highway vagabonds living like hippies
Moving right along to the next big city, okay
Jump off the exit, truck stop, rest stop, next stop Texas
Caravan like a Wild West show
I don't care man as long as we go my way
Get off one and get on the other
Highway vagabonds

Daddy was a drifter, momma died young
And I still don't know where I come from
On the map and off the grid, with all my friends
Roaming town to town like Willie did when he was kid on the road again

Chorus 2:
Highway vagabonds living like hippies
Moving right along to the next big city, okay
Jump off the exit, truck stop, rest stop, next stop Texas
Caravan like a Wild West show
I don't care man as long as we go my way
Singing for your supper
Get off one and get on the other
Highway vagabonds

Well if we ain't broke down then we ain't doing something right
But if we ain't broke down then we ain't slowing down tonight

Highway vagabonds living like hippies
Moving right along to the next big city
Repeat Chorus 2

Highway vagabonds
Living like hippies
Moving right along to the next big city
(Repeat)

Ugly Lights

I dont remember when
the liqar started kicken in
Its been awhile sine Ive been of the stuf
I really hate t say Im turnm into a cliche
I'm hopin that nobody brings it up
I left my car behind the bar again
last sunday night
I did the monday mornm drie of shame
in last nights clothes they smell like smoke
I dont know how I got home
I do know my head will hurt all day

But I still go and stay too late
be the girl bar tenders hate
the one that doesn't need another one
when the romeo and Juliets
have bummed all of my cigareths
last kiss in the parking lot is done
I'll be sittin here alone
when the ugly lights come on

Everybodys got a spark its easy hiding
in the dark
in a cranded room with pockets
full of rings
I sit and watch whisky por the
married men the exit door begging of
anothr matchbook fling
I dont try to clustify the reason I
aint livin right I wer the
sadness like a souvenir
I drint too much to fall apart
thats how I fight a broken
or what if I feel comfortable in here

Ugly Lights

Miranda Lambert/Natalie Hemby/Liz Rose (BMI)

I don't remember when the liquor started kicking in
It's been a while since I've been off the stuff
I really hate to say I'm turning into a cliché
I'm hoping that nobody brings it up
I left my car behind the bar again last Sunday night
I did the Monday morning drive of shame
And last night's clothes they smell smoke
But I don't know how I got home
But I do know my head will hurt all day

Chorus:
But I'll still go and stay too late
And be the girl bartenders hate
The one that doesn't need another one
When the Romeos and Juliets
Have bummed all of my cigarettes
The last kiss in the parking lot is done
I'll be sitting here alone
When the ugly lights come on

Well everybody's got a spark, it's easy hiding in the dark
In a crowded room with pockets full of rings
I sit and watch the whiskey pour, the married men, the exit door
The beginning of another matchbook fling
And I don't try to justify the reason I'm not living right
I wear my sadness like a souvenir
I drink too much to fall apart that's how I fight this broken heart
So what if I feel comfortable in here

Repeat Chorus

You Wouldn't Know Me

Shake Russell (BMI)

You wouldn't know me if you saw me here
Wake up at your front door no more
You'll never know me by askin' how I've been
You'll never keep up that way

Stop sign, stop sign that's all she threw at me
'Til I don't feel like home no more
Wings on fire, I caught sight of a brand new home
Buried in your hills

I told her you wouldn't know me if you saw me here
Wake up at your front door no more
You'll never know me by askin' how I've been
You'll never keep up that way
That's what I say

Bad news is better than what you've been handing me
What's gone wrong with you my friend
Promise me, promise me don't ask that of me now
Won't you just send me some word

I told her you wouldn't know me if you saw me here
I'm changing day to day, that's right
You'll never know me by askin' how I've been
You'll never keep up that way
That's what I say

I told her you wouldn't know me if you saw me here
I'm changing day to day, that's right
You'll never know me by askin' how I've been
You'll never keep up that way

You wouldn't know me
You wouldn't know me

Hey I know ya
bet your minds as
cluttered as yar
kitchen sink
yar herts as empty
as your diesel
tank and any wite
shrt ya ever owned
had a stain

Hey I know ya
ya borran dreses yas borron time
dream all day
drink all night
yr love with love
Down sure ant afraid
to fight
Hey its okay I know
ya

We Should Be Friends

Miranda Lambert (BMI)

If your mind's as cluttered as your kitchen sink
If your heart's as empty as your diesel tank
If all your white t-shirts have stains
If you've got some guts and got some ink, well then
We should be friends

If you borrow dresses like you borrow time
If you dream all day and drink all night
If you're lookin' for love but willin' to fight
Over men and mamas and Miller Lites, well then
We should be friends

I don't know you well but I know that look
And I can judge the cover 'cause I read the book
On losing sleep and gaining weight
On pain and shame and crazy trains

If you paint your nails while you cut your loss
If you like acting like you're the boss
If everything your daddy says is something you can put stock in, well then
We should be friends

I don't know you well but I know that look
And I can judge the cover 'cause I wrote the book
On losing sleep and gaining weight
On pain and shame and crazy trains

1, 2, 3
If use alcohol as a sedative
And "bless you heart" as a negative
If you ride your white horse like the wind
If what you see is what you get, well then
We should be friends, alright

Well then, we should be friends

Pink Sunglasses

Rodney Clawson/Luke Dick/Natalie Hemby (BMI)

I put 'em on whenever I sit down to read the paper
Can't explain the way they seem to work like magic
I put 'em on to keep it positive, don't mean to tell you how to feel
But I'm a firm believer in the power of the plastic
Positive plastic

Chorus:
In my pink sunglasses
Always makes the world look a little bit better
In my pink sunglasses
You can try 'em anytime you need a change of the weather
For $9.99 I'm perfectly disguised
When I'm walkin' by I wanna roll my eyes
In my pink sunglasses
Pink sunglasses

I was lookin' for some tortoise shells but these were on sale
Next to the disposable cameras
Tried 'em on and suddenly it occurred to me
That buyin' Little Debbies felt a little more glamorous
In the checkout line, don't I look good?

Repeat Chorus

I can leave 'em on a beach, at a bar, on a boat
But they always reappear in the pocket of my coat
I can't find them, they always find me

My pink sunglasses
Always makes the world look a little bit better
In my pink sunglasses
You can try 'em anytime you need a change of the weather
For $9.99 I'm completely polarized
Sometimes I accidentally go to bed at night
In my pink sunglasses
My pink sunglasses

Pink sunglasses
(Repeat)

18   ▷ 18A   19   ▷ 19A   20   ▷ 20A

→ ꞬROM THE ꞬRITERS ←

NATALIE HEMBY

It's hard to sum up my feelings for the person who gave me my first shot and changed my life. I love her not just because she believed in me and my writing, but she helped me believe in myself and what I had to say...

I have never connected more musically with an artist than I have with Miranda. She writes what my soul feels...and writing with her leaves you feeling like a song addict...it's so good, you want to write just one more...

LIZ ROSE

Writing with Miranda is like a great night hanging out with a lifelong best friend. She's so honest and open and vulnerable in her songwriting and her artistry. I'm so honored and over the moon to be a part of this record. She is first class! I really love her as a human so much! The writing is a bonus to hanging out!

SHANE MCANALLY

She would absolutely be an in-demand songwriter for every artist in Nashville and beyond, if she wasn't a recording artist. She is unapologetically honest in her songwriting, and her melodic sensibility is as good as anyone I've known. She always makes the co-writing session seamless for everyone in the room, as she lets herself be vulnerable and tells the truth. This is usually a difficult task for a major celebrity, as they try and hide their truth out of fear of anyone seeing beyond their magazine covers. Songs are her therapy, her truth, her lifeline...and, I had an instant kinship with her because that's the reason I write songs: to make it all better. She definitely makes me want to write better, to write truer, and to try and make sense of my crazy thru music.

21   ▷ 21A   22   ▷ 22A   23   ▷ 23A

RODNEY CLAWSON

In my mind Miranda is THE cutting edge
of country music. Her records have fire
and passion and attitude and heart. She's
not scared to let people know who she is
and what she's thinking. When I hear her
music it makes me proud to be from Texas.

LUKE DICK

Miranda is one of those rare artists
that has a bonafide perspective on things
that is real and all her own. When her
soul tugs at her, she listens and heeds.
That's the lifeblood of real songs and
real songwriting. Add all that up, and
crafting a song with Miranda is as great
a creative joy as any.

GWEN SEBASTIAN

Miranda is not only an artist, but a poet
whose message is fearless yet vulnerable
at the same time. I've never met someone
so passionate about creating music that is
important & about uplifting those around
her. I'm honored to be a part of her
journey & even more honored to call her
my friend.

reakin' Hearts & Rollin' Outta

Getaway Driver

Miranda Lambert/Anderson East/Natalie Hemby (BMI)

When she's feelin' reckless
Tangled in her messes
Wild eyes looking for a chase
There's nothing white lines can't erase

Chorus:
So I keep the engine running
She'll be my gasoline
She treats my heart like a stolen car
All the while she had the keys
Standing in the line of fire
I'll be right beside her
I'm her getaway driver
Her getaway driver

Miles were the only thing that saved us
Headlights were our only traces
No rearview mirrors no looking back
Desert horizon as our map

Repeat Chorus

A lover and a fighter
Bonnie and Clyde reminder
I'm her getaway driver
Her getaway driver

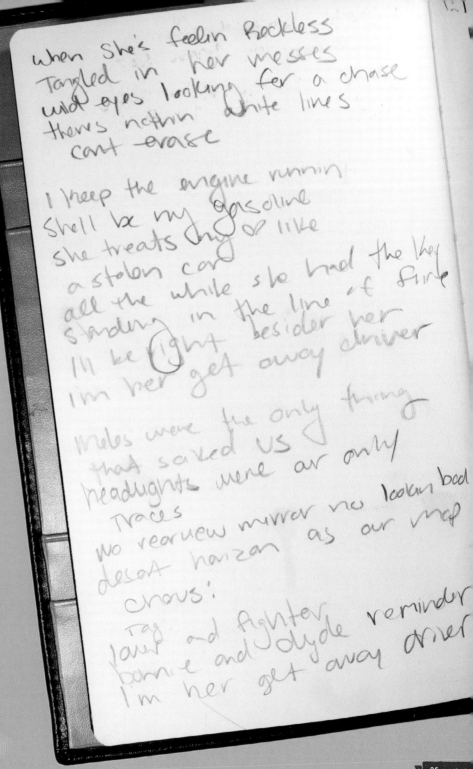

carnival season   Ex boyfriend
                  write's
Vice

sitting of the needle
droppin on the vinyl
neon singer juckbox title
full of heartbreak
B3 45 78   (this)
when it hurts that good
you gotta play it twice
(another vice)

All dressed up in a pretty
black table
sweet salvation on the
dining room table
waitin on me, where the
numb meets the lonely
its gone before it ever melts
the ice, another vice

another call
another bed
I shouldn't crawl
out of at 7 am
shoes in my hand
said I wouldn't do it
but I did it again
I know I'll be back
back tomorrow night

VICE

Miranda Lambert/Shane McAnally/
Josh Osborne (BMI/GMR/ASCAP)

Sting of the needle dropping on a vinyl
Neon singer with a jukebox title
Full of heartbreak
33-45-78
When it hurts this good, you gotta play it twice
Another vice

All dressed up in a pretty black label
Sweet salvation on a dining room table
Waiting on me
Where the numb meets the lonely
It's gone before it ever melts the ice

Another vice, another call
Another bed I shouldn't crawl
Out of at 7am with shoes in my hand
Said I wouldn't do it but I did it again
And I know I'll be back tomorrow night

I wear a town like a leather jacket
When the new wears off I don't even pack it
If you need me
I'll be where my reputation don't precede me
Maybe I'm addicted to goodbyes

Another vice, another town
Where my past can't run me down
Another life, another call
Another bed I shouldn't crawl
Out of at 7am with shoes in my hand
Said I wouldn't do it but I did it again
And I know I'll be gone tomorrow night
Another vice

Standing at the sink not looking in the mirror
Don't know where I am or how I got here
Well the only thing that I know how to find
Is another vice

Another vice
(Repeat)

SMOKING JACKET

Miranda Lambert/Natalie Hemby/
Lucie Silvas (BMI)

Chorus 1:
I want a man with a smoking jacket
And a deeper pocket with money to burn
I want a man who knows his status and he
Makes a habit of loving me 'til it hurts

He might be heavy on the pedal
But he knows how to take it slow
He might be quite continental
But he's sure gonna take me home
Yes he is

Chorus 2:
I want a man with a smoking jacket
And a car that's classic, living bourgeoisie
I want a man whose heart is tragic but he
Makes his magic every night on me

We go together just like
Nicotine and Chanel
And when he lights up I'm his Lucky Strike
Waiting for him to exhale

Repeat Chorus 1

Velvet and refined, he's designed to hold me
I don't need a diamond I like wearing his
smoke rings

I want a man, I want a man

I want a man
I want a man with a smoking jacket and he
Lights his matches with kerosene

I want a man, I want a man
I want a man with a smoking jacket
(Repeat)

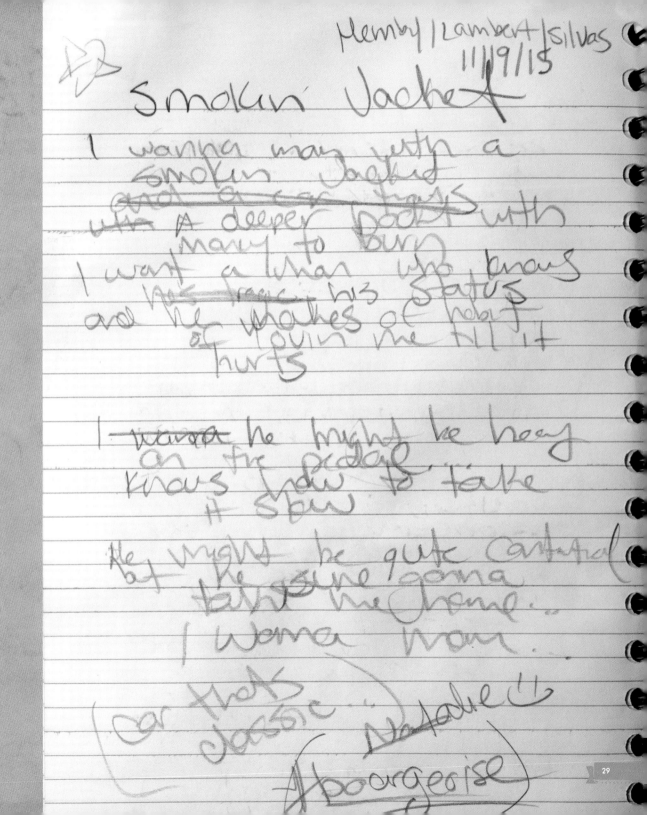

PUSHIN' TIME

Miranda Lambert/Natalie Hemby/Foy Vance (BMI/ASCAP)

Are we fools for rushing in
'Cause I already dread the end
Lonely ain't no place to start
I guess that's just where we are

Oh how I remember well
Sunset on September 12th
I disappeared to get a drink
And you still kept your eyes on me

Chorus:
Sometimes love acts out of spite
And good things happen overnight
Can't take it slow 'cause you and I are pushin' time

I didn't plan on falling fast
I didn't I know could be kissed like that
Now I'm trading miles for minutes
This bed's too big without you in it

Repeat Chorus

You and I are pushin' time

And they say only time can tell
You already know me well
And if it has to end in tears
I hope it's in sixty years

Repeat Chorus

Can't take it slow 'cause you and I are pushin' time

COVERED WAGON

Danny O'Keefe (BMI)

Get the lead out, mama
Pack up everything we own
The smog's about to get me
And I've got a mind to roam

In my covered wagon
Honey, down the road we go
On down the road we go
On down the road we go

I've got an itch to ramble
And I've got no place to be
The people in the city
They ain't got no use for me

In my covered wagon
Mama, down the road we go
On down the road we go
On down the road we go

Baby, down the road we go
On down the road we go
On down the road we go

I'm headed for the country
Can't nothin' keep me here
I feel so free and easy
Like a funky pioneer

In my covered wagon
Mama, down the road we go
On down the road we go
On down the road we go
In my covered wagon
Baby, down the road we go
On down the road we go
Down the road we go
On down the road we go
Baby, down the road we go

On down the road we go
Baby, down the road we go
On down the road we go
Honey, down the road we go

Down the road I go
On down the road we go
(Repeat)

The Nerve to

I can throw a line

The nerve to use
my Heart...

I can throw a line but
I can't reel it in
I can throw a dart
but I can't make
it stick
The thought of lovin
ya just makes
me sick
I don't have the
nerve to use my
heart

I don't have the
nerve to use my
heart

I don't give two
Shits ?

Use My Heart

Miranda Lambert/Ashley Monroe/Waylon Payne (BMI)

I can throw a line but I can't reel it in
I can throw a dart but I can't make it stick
The thought of loving you just makes me sick
I don't have the nerve to use my heart
I don't have the nerve to use my heart

I can write the line but I can't sing the song
I can call my mama but I won't go home
The thought of loving you just makes me sick
I don't have the nerve to use my heart
I don't have the nerve to use my heart

I won't throw a punch but I will turn my cheek
I don't go to church no more but that's what I believe

I don't give two shits no more or so I say
It wouldn't make a difference to you anyway
The thought of loving you just makes me sick
I don't have the nerve to use my heart
I don't have the nerve to use my heart

I don't have the nerve to use my heart
I don't have the nerve to use my heart
(Repeat)

the NOT EXACTLY in CONTROL ROOM

→ FROM THE WRITERS ←

ANDERSON EAST

You could almost say God isn't fair sometimes. For one person or in this case, one woman, to possess so many gifts at once seems otherworldly. The beautiful realization is that those gift aren't kept hidden, they're on display and given so graciously to the world in a way that's natural, effortless and sincere. This world would be a far more beautiful place if there were more people that possessed the heart, talent and most importantly, the love that she does. To know and witness her is a gift I will cherish forever and a day. If any of us are lucky enough to brush up against it, we should consider ourselves lucky.

JOSH OSBORNE

"Miranda's talent in the writing room rivals her talent onstage. I had an incredible experience working with her. She is not an artist just trying to write a song, she is an artist trying to write a great song."

LUCIE SILVAS

Miranda was one of the first artists I heard when I first came to Nashville 2007. My friend, Natalie Hemby, co-wrote "White Liar" with her and it had been playing over in the UK, too. I remember thinking that she represented that same kind of girl power we have in pop; strong females leading the way and with that big distinctive voice. She set the bar for me.

It blew my mind that she heard my music years later and was a fan and then there we were writing together. It was like hanging out with someone I'd known for years and years. She has zero ego and was just excited to get creative and meet new people. An artist like Miranda that can have the success she has had and yet remain so humble and hungry will never hit limits to what she can do. It's all very inspiring.

Coming from completely different backgrounds, we found a common ground as girls doing our thing and wanting to create something new. She isn't afraid to say who she really is and that's my favorite part about her. I love the person she is and she is what country music is all about.

FOY VANCE

"It's easy to see why folks refer to Miranda as country royalty. Every time she opened her mouth to sing she exuded authenticity with a voice soaked in the traditions of country legends."

ASHLEY MONROE

One of the things I love most about Miranda is her artistry. She is like a sister to me, but I still sit back in awe when I watch her carefully piece together her art. From the first phase of writing these amazing songs, to turning it into a record that feels like a chapter in her life. She does it so beautifully. One of the many reasons why she's a gem that will go down in history.

WAYLON PAYNE

I moved back to Nashville in November of 2015. I had been out of any kind of spotlight for quite a few years due to a crippling drug addiction. I decided after about four years of sobriety under my belt to try to get back to work and dive in headfirst. While playing a show one night, I was blown away when I ran into ML. I was even more blown away when she joined me onstage and reminded me through music how healing a song can be. When we sat down a couple of months later to put a pen to paper, I was mesmerized by my friend's ability to bring out such raw emotion from not only her heart, but mine. Music heals. It's the one thing that is true and has never left me. It's really good when you come across a kindred spirit that lets you just "be". I'm very proud of the work that that has been accomplished this year.

Even prouder that the lady with the pink pistol let me join her on this next leg of the journey. Pure and honest, she makes my heart and spirit soar like an eagle when she sings and tells her stories. You guys are gonna be blown away with this one. Love you Miranda. Thanks for sharing some of your heart with ol' Waylon.

THE HEART

THE HEART:
a hollow muscular organ that pumps the blood through the circulatory system by rhythmic   contraction and dilation.
: the central or innermost part
: the essential or most vital part of something or someone
   a. The vital center and source of one's being, emotions, and sensibilities.
   b. The repository of one's deepest and sincerest feelings and beliefs:
   c. The seat of the intellect or imagination

Source: Merriam-Webster's

. . . To lose heart is to stop believing.
To lose YOUR heart is to fall in love . . .
To find your heart is to fall out of love. . .
To follow your heart . . . Is to have the nerve to do so

The heart

- The hands that shake while he is lighting my cigarette in the city.

- The sigh of relief ... the hardest part is almost over

- The eyes that twitch but look for beauty in every dark moment ugly

- The mind that lays awake and counts the clicks of a _____

The heart...
the hardest love.
the place to always
go back to.
the one th chase
The one

The heart,

it leads chase
it follows
its full, it's hollow
it breaks like a
mm wine glass in
a full dishwasher
it brings joy

Tin man

Hey there mr. Tin man
you don't know how
lucky you are
shouldn't spend your whole
life wishin
for something bound to
fall apart
everytime you feelin
empty

Thank your luck stars
Take it from me darling
you don't want
a heart

Tin Man

Miranda Lambert/Jack Ingram/Jon Randall (BMI)

Hey there mister tin man
You don't know how lucky you are
You shouldn't spend your whole life wishin'
For something bound to fall apart
Every time you're feeling empty
Better thank your lucky stars
If you ever felt one breakin'
You'd never want a heart

Ooh, ooh, ooh

Hey there mister tin man
You don't know how lucky you are
I've been on the road that you're on
It didn't get me very far
You ain't missin' nothing
'Cause love is so damn hard
Take it from me darlin'
You don't want a heart

Ooh, ooh, ooh
Ooh, ooh, ooh

Hey there mister tin man
I'm glad we talked this out
You can take mine if you want it
It's in pieces now
By the way there mister tin man
If you don't mind the scars
You give me your armor
And you can have my heart

Ooh, ooh, ooh
(Repeat)

Good Ol' Days

Miranda Lambert/Brent Cobb/Adam Hood (BMI)

Oh southern breeze knock me to my knees
I believe you're the only one who can
The religious and the rest they've all tried their best
Well I guess some things you just don't understand

Chorus:
Oh Lord, when will the road run out
I'm on a roll but I'm in doubt
And I don't know why still I second guess my pace
If I stand to lose from winning
To find the truth I'm willing
To start back at the beginning of the good ol' days
The good ol' days

Oh southern pines reaching for the sky
I'm convinced that I can fly beneath your shade
And it's long overdue spending time just me and you
The pulpit and the pew where I was saved

Repeat Chorus twice

Oh southern breeze knock me to my knees
I believe you're the only one who can

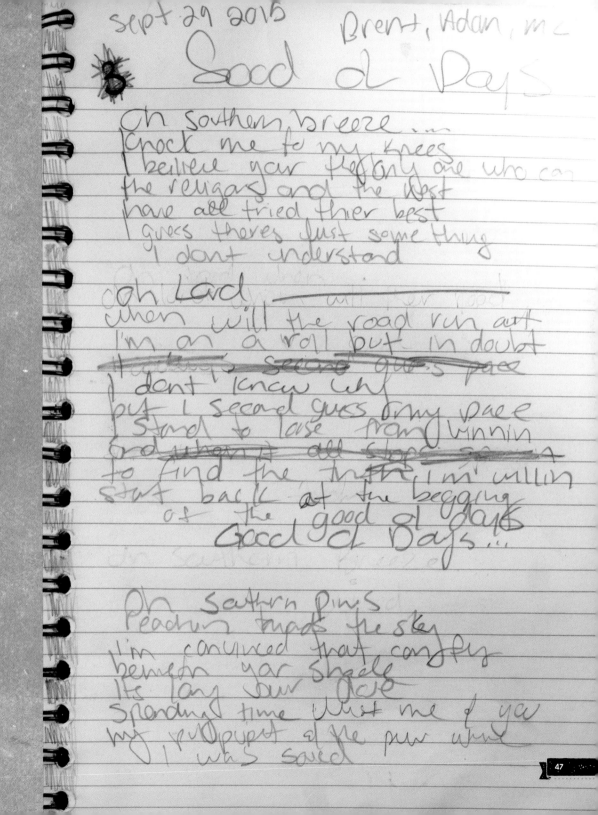

CHINGS CHAT BREAK

Miranda Lambert/Jessi Alexander/Natalie Hemby
(BMI/ASCAP)

I was born a bull in a china cabinet
Drawn to the delicate like it's a magnet
Perfume bottles on a mirror tray
Tempered glass on a window pane
Timeless face on a pocket watch
Time is ticking

Chorus:
I'll leave it all in ruins
'Cause I don't know what I'm doing
I'm hard on things that matter
Hold a heart so tight it shatters
So I stay away
From things that break

I can't make a man a promise with the best of intentions
Or drive two hundred miles on a run-down engine
Put a blanket underneath a hollow tree
When the wind blows hard it'll fall on me
Stick around long enough and you will see
Time is ticking

Repeat Chorus

Me, I don't ever wanna get too close
Or be held responsible
For all the pain that you can't see
Somebody once broke me

Repeat Chorus

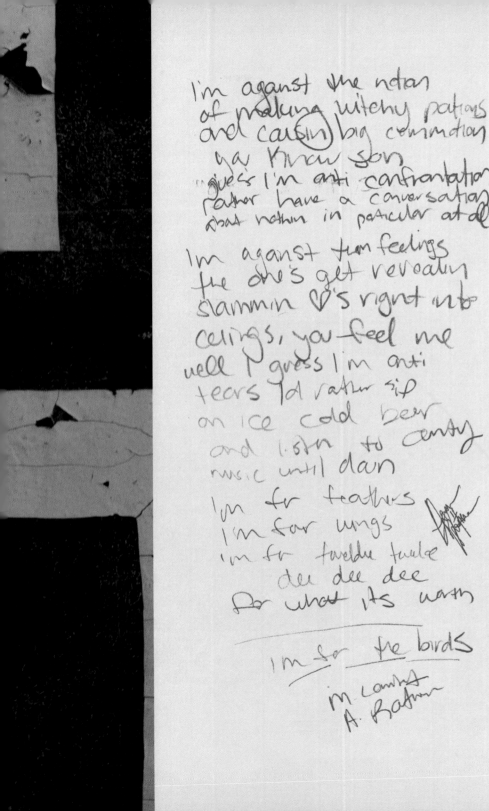

FOR THE BIRDS

Miranda Lambert/Aaron Raitiere (BMI)

I'm against the days
When the skies stay bummer grey
And the cake tastes just okay, okay
Well I guess I'm anti-yuck
Against the stuff that sucks
The life out of your soul and shuts it down

I'm against the thought
Of letting good tomatoes rot
Being someone that you're not, when you're not
Well I guess I'm anti-hate
'Cause that ain't what it takes
It's love that makes this crazy world go 'round

I'm for the sun, I'm for the breeze
Old dogs sleeping at your feet
I'm for the girls with the curls and the curves
I'm for questions, I'm for freedom
Celebrating every season
For the bees and the trees and the dirt
I'm for the birds
I'm for the birds
I'm for the birds

I'm against the notion
Of drinking witchy potions
And causing big commotion, you know son
I guess I'm anti-confrontation
I'd rather have a conversation
About nothing in particular at all

I'm against them feelin's
The ones that get revealin'
Slamming hearts right into ceilings, you feel me
And I guess I'm anti-tears
I'd rather sip an ice cold beer
Listen to some country music until dawn

'Cause I'm for the sun, I'm for the breeze
Old dogs sleeping at your feet
I'm for the girls with the curls and the curves
I'm for questions, I'm for freedom
Celebrating every season
For the trees and the bees and the dirt
I'm for feathers, I'm for wings, I'm for tweedle
deedle dee dee dee
For what it's worth, for what it's worth
I'm for the birds

I'm for the birds
(Repeat)

Tweedle deedle dee dee dee

Well Rested

This moment is heavy
for me I'm not ready
like a caged bird barely
set free
forgive me I'm finding
my wings

It's your tail that
your chasin
it's the past I'm erasing
but your heart can't be
tested
when it can't
well rested

Forgive me I'm finding
my wings....

WELL-RESTED

*Miranda Lambert/Anderson East/
Aaron Raitiere (BMI)*

Well this moment is heavy
For me I'm not ready
Like a caged bird barely set free
Forgive me I'm finding my wings

While my body is present
My heart is absent
And my mind is racing
My feet are pacing

Chorus 1:
It's your tail you're chasing
It's the past I'm erasing
And your heart can't be tested
When it ain't well-rested

My gears are grinding
I'm leaving, you're arriving
It's a matter of timing
I guess loving ain't surviving

Chorus 2:
It's your tail that you're chasing
It's the past I'm erasing
And a heart can't be tested
When it ain't well-rested

Repeat Chorus 2

Don't waste your investment
If my heart ain't well-rested
My heart ain't well-rested

Tomboy

Miranda Lambert/Natalie Hemby/Aaron Raitiere (BMI)

Tomboy, Hail Mary
Never needs a dress to make her pretty
She's a killjoy, such a let down
Daddy tried to raise a southern belle
Well, he got a tomboy

Tomboy, in between
Dirt in her nails and holes in her jeans
She'll destroy all your dreams
And ride out like a rodeo queen
Know what I mean, she's a tomboy

Tangled hair and bruises on her knees
She wears her scars outside her sleeves
Always has a way of saying no way
Some people don't get her but that's okay
Move along boy, she's a tomboy

Barfly, bad Betty
Band of brothers that got her back
She's unladylike like a scout fire
Got her own constellation in the zodiac
Well who can say that, a tomboy

Tangled hair and bruises on her knees
She's hard to love and hard to please
Always has a way of saying no way
Some people don't get her but that's okay
Move along boy, she's a tomboy

Ooh, ooh, ooh, ooh
Ooh, ooh, ooh, ooh

She's got a softer side she'll never let you see
With tears in her eyes she'd rather be caught dead
A sweet contradiction with no guarantees
She is what she is, you get what you get
Move along boy, she's a tomboy
Or go along with it boy, you got a tomboy

55

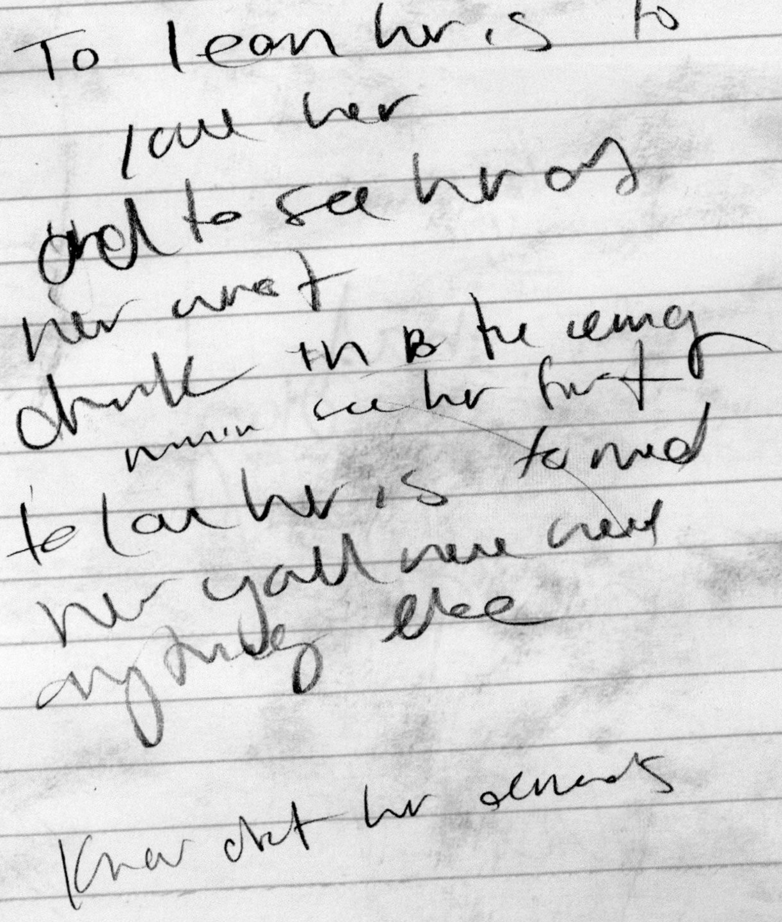

[Handwritten draft lyrics, partially legible:]

To learn her is to
love her
and to see her at
her worst
drunk ... to be ...
... see her hurt
to love her is to learn
her you'll never know
anything else

Know that her always

To Learn Her

Miranda Lambert/Ashley Monroe/Waylon Payne (BMI)

To love her is to learn her
And see her at her worst
Dance with her when she's drinkin'
Hold her when she hurts
She'll be happy, you'll be sorry
Well that's just how it works
To love her is to learn her
Some things you just can't learn

You'll her meet her mama, you'll love her daddy
You'll know how much she's worth
You'll have Thanksgiving dinners
And Sunday morning church
You'll be true and you'll be tried
But the tables always turn
To love her is to learn her
Some things you just can't learn

It's a lesson, it's a blessin'
You don't know everything
If you take her you might hate her
And be left with just a ring

To love her is to lose her
Hey, that's just how it works
To love her is to learn her
Some things you just can't learn

Oh to love her is to learn her
Some things you just can't learn

M. Lambert

[handwritten draft notes]

KEEPER OF THE FLAME

Miranda Lambert/Natalie Hemby/Liz Rose (BMI)

I'm walking in their footsteps, I'm singing their old songs
Somebody blazed this trail I'm treading on
I'm bent but I'm not broken, I'm stronger than I feel
I'm made of flesh and bone, not made of steel

Chorus:
I'm the keeper of the flame, the teller of the story
Keeper of the flame for the ones that came before me
For the little pilot lights waiting to ignite
Like fireflies in the rain, keeper of the flame

I've been burned down to ashes waiting for a wind
To carry me and start a fire again
Sometimes I'm just a flicker, a candle in your eye
But I swear to God I'll never let it die

Repeat Chorus

When I'm drowning, when I'm fighting
When I'm screaming, when I'm hiding
When I'm losin', when I'm winnin'
I go back to the beginning

Keeper of the flame, the teller of the story
Keeper of the flame I'm not doing it for the glory
But for those little pilot lights waiting to ignite
Like fireflies in the rain, keeper of the flame

I'm the keeper of the flame
I'm the keeper of the flame

→ FROM THE WRITERS ←

JACK INGRAM

1. First time I saw Miranda Lambert play was OUTSIDE of Nacodogches, Texas opening up a small music festival (it was outside of Nac!)...I was sitting in a van and said "Who's THAT?!" I marched to the front of the stage to listen. I knew right then, as I know now, that she would be an artist who could and would make a difference. I also knew that she never needed to wonder who her 3rd biggest fan is...
1. Rick L,
2. Beverly L,
3. That would be me!

2. Country Stars can come & go and we thank them for the effort...but true artists - the rare gifts like Miranda...are the ones who provide the light that everybody else uses for reflection!

3. Miranda used to drive to the ends of Texas to sneak in the Honky Tonks & watch me play. First time I saw her play I knew I would be going to the ends of the earth just to keep up with her!

4. Did I mention how much I love her...it's a lot.

JON RANDALL

Miranda Lambert is the "The Real Damned Deal" across the board. As a person, artist, songwriter and friend. One of the hardest working people I know. She knows who she is and what's she believes without wavering. That's rare in the music business these days."

BRENT COBB

In a word and in the true sense of that word, Miranda is an ARTIST. In my experience with her, she is an inspired songwriter/artist who purely follows her heart. Thank God for that.

JESSI ALEXANDER

Miranda continues to inspire me as a musician, friend and songwriter. She follows her truth even when its a risk and raises the bar for all of us.

ADAM HOOD

The thing that I admire most about Miranda is that she's steadily worked her way to the top of country music using great songs as her main tool. She won't settle when it comes to the songs she writes and songs by other writers she chooses to record. There's no filler. No throw away's. That commitment has been at the front of what she does as long as I've known her. I am one of many people that is thankful that she always chooses the integrity of music. Her honest songwriting is a gift that everyone can relate to.

AARON RAITIERE

Writing with Miranda is like finding out your best friend has a hidden life as a professor: she approaches people with humility and humor, but with wisdom too. She can lead a song down lots of different roads, but she also listens and allows the song to lead itself. Every bit of energy she commits to the creative process is a sweet musical gift to the world.

Bad Boy

Miranda Lambert/Mando Saenz (BMI/ASCAP)

Saturday's gonna keep you up all night
'Cause Sunday morning ain't your style
It's been awhile since I've seen the sunrise
I'm not sure how you make your livin'
You can buy me one of whatever you're drinkin'
I'm thinking my mama warned me about your kind

Sure you can light my cigarette
Don't think you can light my heart
Don't think I hadn't figured you out from the start
Giving in to bad boys like you never got me very far
It's trouble now, baby drink it down
Oh you should have seen it coming

Bad boy, drivin' me mad boy
I got it bad boy for you
Bad boy, maybe it's a bad choice
I got it bad boy for you

The more I hear your silence speak
The more my curiosity piques
The more I don't wanna leave this bar alone
The whiskey's making me wonder why
You wear your hat down low but your walls are high
How long you gonna hide behind them walls of stone

Sure you can buy me one more round
Don't think you can buy my heart
Don't think I hadn't figured you out from the start
Giving in to bad boys like you never got me very far
It's trouble now, baby drink it down
Oh you should have seen it coming

Bad boy, drivin' me mad boy
I got it bad boy for you
Bad boy, maybe it's a bad choice
I got it bad boy, bad boy for you

Oh you should have seen it coming
Bad boy, drivin' me mad boy
I got it bad boy for you
Bad boy, maybe it's a bad choice
I got it bad boy, bad boy

Bad boy, drivin' me mad boy
I got it bad boy, bad boy

Read More, Write More
More, EAT MORE
Laugh More, Love More,
... More, DRAW More
WORRY LESS.

4.20.16

BAD BOY   mando
                 seanz

Saturdays gonna keep
ya up all night
cause sunday mornin aint
your style its been awhile
since I've seen the
    sunrise

I'm not sure how you
make yar livin you
can buy me and of
whatever your drinkin
I'm thinkin my mama
warned me bout yar kind

Sure ya can light my
    cigarette
dont think ya can
light my heart
dont think I hadnt
figured ya out
from the start

6 degrees of
separation

were all over this
damn nation

I'm ~~out of my~~
ever out of my reach
geographically

ya still find a
way to get ahold
of me

6 degrees of separation
oh oh oh

hailed a cab up in NYC
saw an add for a
litigation lawer on a
bus stop bench
sittin watin for the
red light to turn
green 'smoke
breakers flirtin on
the steps of merril

SIX DEGREES OF SEPARATION

Miranda Lambert/Nicolle Galyon/Natalie Hemby (BMI)

Thought that I was safe down in New Orleans
'Til I picked up a quarter from 1979
Stuck it in the back pocket of these jeans
Worn-in boyfriend button-down Levi's
In a saint's town I can't seem figure out
How to get around but I ain't moving on
Threw the quarter in an old street case
And I'll be damned, he started playing our song

Chorus:
Six degrees of separation
You're all over this damn nation
Well I'm out of your reach geographically
But you still find a way to get a hold of me
And it's six degrees of separation
Whoa, whoa-oh, whoa, whoa-oh

Hailed a cab up in NYC
Saw an ad for a litigation lawyer on a bus stop bench
Sitting waiting for the red light to turn green
Smoke breakers flirtin' on the steps of Merrill Lynch
Hit the Roosevelt took it to the 12th
Got a funny feeling as I put my key in the door
Never seen the likes of these city lights
I swear to God, son, I've been here before

Repeat Chorus

Well it's six degrees of separation
Yeah it's six degrees of separation
Thought that I was safe down in New Orleans
'Til I picked up a quarter from 1979

Dear Old Sun

Miranda Lambert/Terri Jo Box/Gwen Sebastian
(BMI/ASCAP)

Dear old sun
How you holdin' up?
Through the winter cold
Up there all alone
February's been hard on a heart
But we're near the end and it's almost March
Though the sky's been grey
And in our way
I still see your light

Well you melt the snow
And you grow the roses
And you dry the tears
And you freckle noses
Our little world revolves around
You coming up and goin' down

Oooh, oooh

Dear old sun
Let's call it a day
And I'll watch you set
And I'll let you rest
But I'll wait for you
Like mornin's do
'Til I see your light

Oooh, oooh, oooh

I still see your light
I still see your light
Heaven shinin' down tonight
I still see your light

I still see your light
I still see your light
Heaven shinin' down tonight
I still see your light

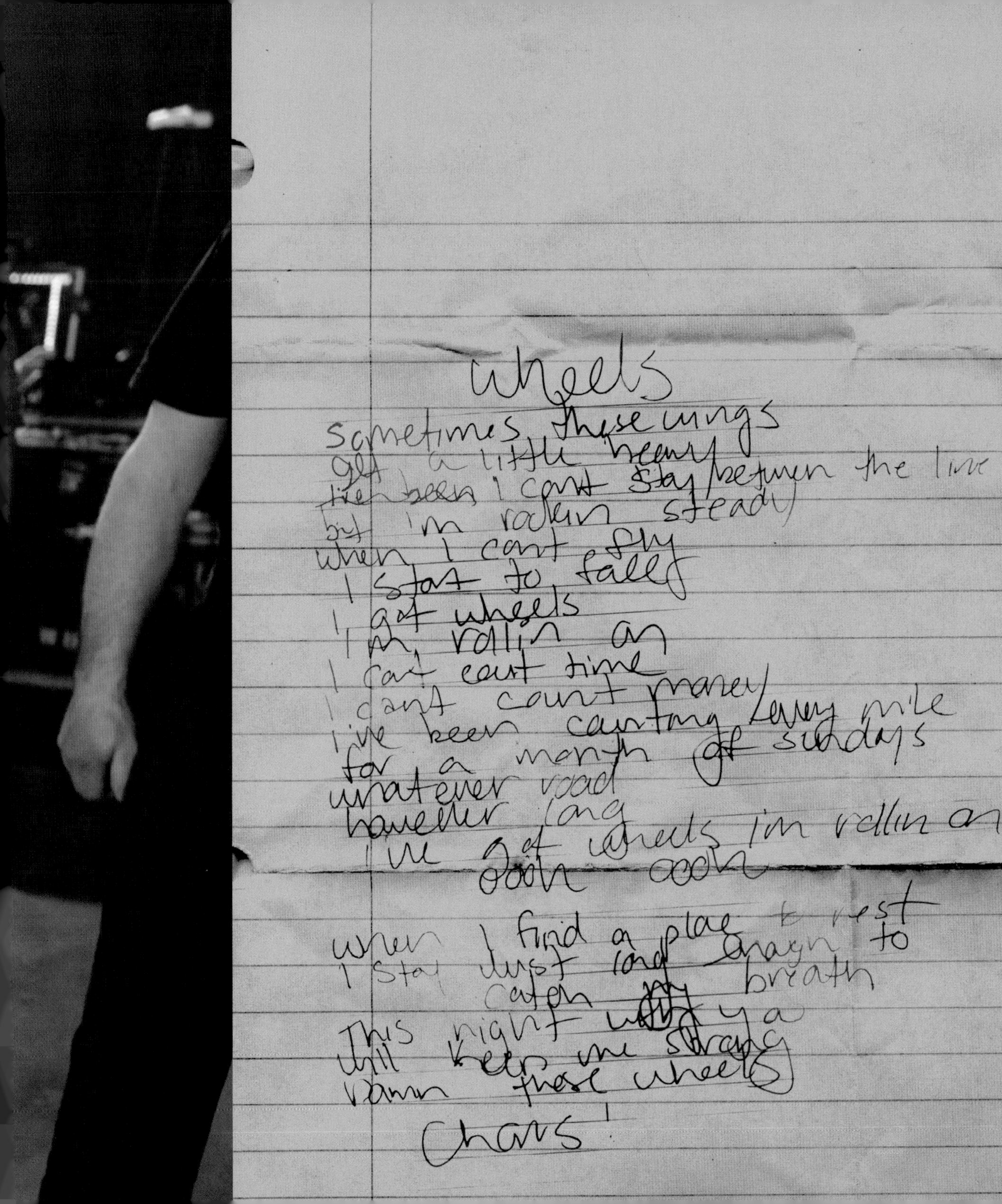

I've Got Wheels

Miranda Lambert/Gwen Sebastian/Scotty Wray (BMI/ASCAP)

Chorus:
Sometimes these wings get a little heavy
I can't stay between the lines but I'm rockin' steady
When I can't fly I start to fall
But I've got wheels I'm rolling on

I can't count time
I can't count money
But I've been counting every mile for a month of Sundays
Whatever road however long
I've got wheels I'm rolling on

Repeat Chorus

And when I find a place to rest
I stay just long enough to catch my breath
This night with you will keep me strong
Damn these wheels I'm rolling on

Repeat Chorus

I've got wheels, I've got wheels
(Repeat)

→ FROM THE WRITERS ←

MANDO SAENZ

I've known Miranda for a while but just recently had the opportunity to work with her and get to know her better. I've always been a fan but now I see more of why her music is able to connect with so many people. I think it's because she is genuinely one of the people. Very down to earth, honest and real, which comes through in her music. She's someone they can relate to, and that resonates loudly. And at the end of the day, she's just a truly talented songwriter with not only a great voice, but distinctive one as well. It was such a pleasure to write with her. She's fun to drink a beer with too!

NICOLLE GALYON

Writing with Miranda feels like a free pass to go everywhere you might be afraid to go with someone else. She makes you feel like you don't have to ask permission to say anything - like the perfect balance of honesty and bravery.

SCOTTY WRAY

First off, any time I've ever spent with Miranda has been time well spent...Be it a minute or hours...Writing with her is a breeze...She has a quick and witty mind. I LOVE her with all my heart.

TERRI JO BOX

Miranda makes everything count. Whether it's a song, a joke, a workout, a friend, a fan, a good movie, or a drink, she doesn't waste fun...or pain. She lives in her moment and celebrates yours. She'll out write, out sing and out wit you, all while she's cooking you something to eat. Miranda Lambert is one of the greatest artist music has ever had. She is a jewel, a genius, an icon, and a legend...but somebody forgot to tell her. Love you ML

→ FROM THE STUDIO ←

GLENN WORF
Bass/Co-Producer

I've been lucky enough to work with three generations of artists now, a fair number of whom are among the greatest of all time. With this new record, I believe Miranda has taken her place with the best of them. Her music is brave, brilliant, and brutally honest; the kind that only the highest caliber artists achieve. I am honored and humbled to have been able join in the making of it.

LUKE REYNOLDS
Electric Guitar/Piano/Synth

I think it's a testament to the kind of artist Miranda is, that she made a record this raw, fearless and wide open. Her confidence and fearlessness to push boundaries, helped unite the studio band. She encouraged us to take risks stretch into place which was easy with songs that good in a team that fearless.

Credit goes to my Miranda's openness to work with new and outside players, and Frank Liddell for going to bat to have me on this record. I put everything I had into it.

I'm real proud of the work we did the decisions we made in how are raw the spirit of this record feels, given the current backdrop of the majority of what passes for country music.

SPENCER CULLUM
Steel Guitar

I'm so very proud to have been apart of this new Miranda Lambert record. Going into a studio environment where every musician pushes themselves emotionally and challenges the way they play, due to the very high level of craftsmanship and honesty by the artist is one of the reasons I wanted to become a musician. It's how records should be made, especially in this day and age.

Its timeless, raw and a deeply honest. That's the greatest kind of music to me.

MATT CHAMBERLAIN
Drums/Percussion

This is the third record I've done with Miranda, it's always a blast and she is such a great singer and great person to hang with. I love working with her because she is all about vibe, if the take isn't perfect but the vibe is right that's all that matters to her, which is so right on. The other great thing about her, is she is always looking to try different ways to make her songs special--she let's us do a lot of searching for the right sounds, grooves, parts, etc to make her music, her music! I really think this new record we just cut is her best one yet, I love the songs and the laid back way we tracked everything (in Eric Masse's garage) lended itself to thinking outside the box...I'm really looking forward to hearing this record all finished...
Viva Miranda! :)

FRANK RISCHE
Acoustic & Electric Guitar

Real music. A phrase tossed around in this business as it goes in and out of style. Miranda's music will be relevant from now till then, and then on. With powerful material, great pride comes with the experience I had making this album. She is a true classic.

ERIC MASSE
Co-Producer/Engineer

Miranda is one of the smartest and most gifted artists of our time. Her songwriting doesn't turn and look away, it stares you right in the heart and uncovers all of your deepest secrets. The songs she wrote for this project are some of the most honest songs I've ever heard and they truly represent the person and friend I've come to know. She is brave, and she is kind. I feel humbled and grateful to be a part of her journey, and I am constantly wowed by her artistry and grace. Miranda is one of this country's finest jewels, and her new songs are like a pick axe to my heart.

CHRIS TAYLOR

Miranda is genuine. In addition to her unique and prolific musical talent there is a connection to her music that is almost inescapable because of it's honesty. And that sincerity is definitely not confined to her music. She's an incredibly kind and gracious person as well.

iranda came to me over a year ago and said 'I'm going through a lot in my life right now, I have a lot on my mind and a lot in my heart, I want to live it, experience it and I want to write about it all.' Miranda has always had this uncanny knack for leaving an old record behind and not staring at it in the rear view as we created a new one. So, fresh off of a successful record by many standards, she told me respectfully, that nothing she had done before was sacred. I knew this record would be different, not different from the previous one as the others had been, different from all of them.

Natalie, Blu, Mando, Ashley, Mike, Gwen, Jon, Jack, Brent, Shane ...We talked about how to begin and it was obvious that we had to start with the song. So she started writing, I started thinking. And she wrote a lot and I thought a lot.

The garage. When I look back on this record it seems like the whole thing was mapped out logically but it wasn't. We started off last summer with a rag-tag group of folks in a garage on Greenwood, Eric, Frank, Chris, Lex, Miranda, Sarah, Sarah, Brittany and me. We just plowed through with one goal, to find a pulse, a heartbeat. Time went by, seasons changed, she wrote more, I thought more, we recorded more. Glenn came back and ultimately Matt, Luke and Spencer. We scrapped all recording plans of grandeur and never left the garage. For a year. Marion and Crystal joined us and sooner or later Joey (who thought he might be in the wrong place) came by to see what he had fostered and Duane came by to see what he was paying for. There were beers, tacos, failed attempts at fires, fires that burned, Crazy Ricky, beers, Lord C, charcuterie at one point, tears, laughter, emotion, more thought, confusion, highs and lows. There were arguments for sure, and a time for a second where I thought we might be scrapping everything and moving on with our separate lives. We were just scared, there's nothing wrong with that. Each of us was looking inside for something more, something different, something of ourselves that we knew we had in us but had never tapped into. After all, this was the lonely record.

The first song on the Nerve is 'Running Just in Case'. When we started this record, it was hot and humid and all was green, it was summer, the world and Mother Nature were running, not toward anything not from anything, just as they do, just in case. Soon the leaves turned golden and then brown and then fell to the ground and the fires came and there were vices and smoking jackets and things that break and we were pushing time and trying to come up with the nerve to use our hearts to make a difference. And sooner or later the dear old sun came up again a little warmer, again, as it does and the peach tree started budding, the flowers bloomed, the spring showers blew in, we had kept the flame and were still friends. And then once again, it was hot and humid and we hadn't moved, but we had found the Nerve and the Heart. The final song on the Heart is Wheels. Just like we rolled in we rolled out. This record has no beginning and no end, it is a reflection of one life in a lonely time and window to a brief chapter about a confluence of lives.

The last day of overdubs found us standing outside the garage all together for the last time. We were talking and laughing about what we had done and how to make sense of it in mixing. We were all about to go our separate ways, as we all have other lives and other jobs to get on with. We were in good spirits, and Glenn said that he would miss us and 'this'. He was being cordial but I could sense something deeper, that we would all miss each other, and 'this'. I knew an important time in each of our lives was drawing to a close, something special was coming to an end: Something beyond just the music, that chapter of which I earlier wrote. That chapter in our lives is in this record and that's what warms my heart the most. When we do something right, we know it, it feels good. I wish I could tell each of you what you mean to me, and what you mean to this record and what this record means to me. I might never be able to bring myself to do so, but let's just say as I sit here, I miss the garage.

Glenn is a world-traveling musician and one of my favorite things in life is getting texts from him wherever he might be, indicating that he is drinking a glass of wine and tilting it in my direction. It is a sign that all somehow is well. As I wind this up, I have a glass of wine that I will tilt in each and all of your directions. I'm feeling a bit lonely, but this is the lonely record: Here's to the lonely record, to you ML and to the rest of you...

– FRANK LIDDELL
(PRODUCER)

BEVERLY LAMBERT

I've heard that you learn more about yourself through your child, truth is that I learn from Miranda every day. I learn by watching her business skills, her compassionate heart, her management style and her artistic eye. But I learn the most about myself through her lyrics. Too many times to count I have listened to her music and realized that she said something I had always thought or felt OR something that I've never thought or felt! So often I hear phrases like "She was looking right through me" or "That song went right to my soul". That's because she writes about how people feel... about common experiences and emotions that humans share. Then she delivers the message with integrity and conviction and we all feel understood. We all feel some kind of ownership and we feel like we've learned something about ourselves.

RICK LAMBERT

We were driving home from Nashville where 16-year-old Miranda had just recorded a mini-album, which we self-funded with a borrowed $6,000. The songs were age appropriate, but very girly pop-py and indicative of what was coming out of the music machine at the time. Listening to the disc on the way home, Miranda burst into tears and said "Daddy, that's not who I am at all". A little surprised, I pointed at my heart and said "Baby, this is who you are and only you can let it out. Writing your own songs is the way you do that". I think that's the day the transformation to Miranda Lambert, the ARTIST, began. I am constantly overwhelmed, amazed and very proud of what my little formerly shy, introspective daughter has given to the world by baring her own soul.

LUKE LAMBERT

Something I most admire about my sister is her unwavering commitment to her craft. After over a decade of creating music, I imagine it's easy to become complacent or distracted by the trappings of success, but Miranda has always been focused on one goal: telling stories that tap into universal experiences and resonate with listeners from all different backgrounds. Every decision she makes is guided by the desire to create great art. To be sure, each album brings an evolution of sound and personal growth, but there's a connective tissue of an artist remaining true to herself. I'm so proud that the Miranda I know today is still the same one I grew up with in the house that built me.

WANDA COKER (NONNY)

Songwriting, singing and performing...Miranda has the talent to do all three and do it well. I am so proud of her. She has done a great job with the gifts that God gave her.

1. TIN MAN
Miranda Lambert/Jack Ingram/ Jon Randall (BMI)
© 2016 Sony/ATV Tree Publishing/Pink Dog Publishing (BMI). All rights adm by Sony/ATV Music Publishing LLC, 424 Church Street, Suite 1200, Nashville, TN 37219. © 2016 JACK INGRAM PUBLISHER DESIGNEE. © 2016 BMG Platinum Songs (BMI)/ SWMBMGBMI/Lonesome Vinyl Music. All rights adm by BMG Rights Management (US) LLC. Used by permission. All rights reserved.

2. GOOD OL' DAYS
Miranda Lambert/Brent Cobb/ Adam Hood (BMI)
© 2016 Sony/ATV Tree Publishing/Pink Dog Publishing (BMI). All rights adm by Sony/ATV Music Publishing LLC, 424 Church Street, Suite 1200, Nashville, TN 37219. © 2016 Tiltawhirl Music (BMI). A division of Carnival Music Group. © 2016 Warner-Tamerlane Publishing Corp./AlaTex Music/Super LCS Publishing (BMI). All rights adm by Warner-Tamerlane Publishing Corp. Used by permission. All rights reserved.

3. THINGS THAT BREAK
Miranda Lambert/Jessi Alexander/ Natalie Hemby (BMI/ASCAP)
© 2016 Sony/ATV Tree Publishing/Pink Dog Publishing (BMI). All rights adm by Sony/ATV Music Publishing LLC,

424 Church Street, Suite 1200, Nashville, TN 37219. © 2016 WB Music Corp./Party of Five Music/Thankful For This Music (ASCAP). All rights adm by WB Music Corp. © 2016 Happygowrucke/Creative Pulse Music/These Are Pulse Songs (BMI). All rights adm by These Are Pulse Songs.

4. FOR THE BIRDS
Miranda Lambert/Aaron Raitiere (BMI)
© 2016 Sony/ATV Tree Publishing/Pink Dog Publishing (BMI). All rights adm by Sony/ATV Music Publishing LLC, 424 Church Street, Suite 1200, Nashville, TN 37219. © 2016 Warner-Tamerlane Publishing Corp./One Tooth Productions/ Super LCS Publishing (BMI). All rights adm by Warner-Tamerlane Publishing Corp.

5. WELL-RESTED
Miranda Lambert/Anderson East/ Aaron Raitiere (BMI)
© 2016 Sony/ATV Tree Publishing/ Pink Dog Publishing (BMI). All rights adm by Sony/ATV Music Publishing LLC, 424 Church Street, Suite 1200, Nashville, TN 37219. © 2016 Farmland Music (BMI). All rights adm by Songs of Kobalt Music Publishing. © 2016 Warner-Tamerlane Publishing Corp./One Tooth Productions/Super LCS Publishing (BMI). All rights adm by Warner-Tamerlane Publishing Corp.

6. TOMBOY
Miranda Lambert/Natalie Hemby/ Aaron Raitiere (BMI)
© 2016 Sony/ATV Tree Publishing/ Pink Dog Publishing (BMI). All rights adm by Sony/ATV Music Publishing LLC, 424 Church Street, Suite 1200, Nashville, TN 37219. © 2016 Happygowrucke/Creative Pulse Music/These Are Pulse Songs (BMI). All rights adm by These Are Pulse Songs. © 2016 Warner-Tamerlane Publishing Corp./One Tooth Productions/Super LCS Publishing (BMI). All rights adm by Warner-Tamerlane Publishing Corp.

7. TO LEARN HER
Miranda Lambert/Ashley Monroe/ Waylon Payne (BMI)
© 2016 Sony/ATV Tree Publishing/Pink Dog Publishing (BMI). All rights adm by Sony/ATV Music Publishing LLC, 424 Church Street, Suite 1200, Nashville, TN 37219. © 2016 Monroe Suede Publishing (BMI), All rights adm by Songs of Kobalt Music Publishing. © 2016 Tiltawhirl Music (BMI). A division of Carnival Music Group. Used by permission. All rights reserved.

8. KEEPER OF THE FLAME
Miranda Lambert/Natalie Hemby/ Liz Rose (BMI)
© 2016 Sony/ATV Tree Publishing/Pink Dog Publishing (BMI). All rights adm by Sony/ATV Music Publishing LLC, 424 Church Street, Suite 1200, Nashville, TN 37219. © 2016 Happygowrucke/Creative Pulse

Songs/These Are Pulse Songs (BMI). All rights adm by These Are Pulse Songs. © 2016 Warner-Tamerlane Publishing Corp./Songs of Crazy Girl Music (BMI). All rights adm by Warner-Tamerlane Publishing Corp.

9. BAD BOY
Miranda Lambert/Mando Saenz (BMI/ASCAP)
© 2016 Sony/ATV Tree Publishing/Pink Dog Publishing (BMI). All rights adm by Sony/ATV Music Publishing LLC, 424 Church Street, Suite 1200, Nashville, TN 37219. © 2016 Scrambler Music (ASCAP). A division of Carnival Music Group. Used by permission. All rights reserved.

10. SIX DEGREES OF SEPARATION
Miranda Lambert/Nicolle Galyon/ Natalie Hemby (BMI)
© 2016 Sony/ATV Tree Publishing/Pink Dog Publishing (BMI). All rights adm by Sony/ATV Music Publishing LLC, 424 Church Street, Suite 1200, Nashville, TN 37219. © 2016 Warner-Tamerlane Publishing Corp./A Girl Named Charlie (BMI). All rights adm by Warner-Tamerlane Publishing Corp. © 2016 Happygowrucke/Creative Pulse Music/These Are Pulse Songs (BMI). All rights adm by These Are Pulse Songs.

11. DEAR OLD SUN
Miranda Lambert/Terri Jo Box/ Gwen Sebastian (BMI/ASCAP)
© 2016 Sony/ATV Tree Publishing/Pink Dog Publishing (BMI). All rights adm by Sony/ATV Music Publishing LLC, 424 Church Street, Suite 1200, Nashville, TN 37219. © 2016 Songs Of Merf Music, LLC (ASCAP). © 2016 Music of Open Road (ASCAP) adm by Words & Music, a division of Big Deal Music, LLC. All rights reserved. Used by permission. International copyright secured.

12. I'VE GOT WHEELS
Miranda Lambert/Gwen Sebastian/ Scotty Wray (BMI/ASCAP)
© 2016 Sony/ATV Tree Publishing/Pink Dog Publishing (BMI). All rights adm by Sony/ATV Music Publishing LLC, 424 Church Street, Suite 1200, Nashville, TN 37219. © 2016 Music of Open Road (ASCAP) adm by Words & Music, a division of Big Deal Music, LLC. © 2016 Saraway Music (BMI). All rights reserved. Used by permission. International copyright secured.